LIFE OUGHT TO COME WITH DIRECTIONS

LIFE OUGHT TO COME WITH DIRECTIONS

JEFF & RAMONA
TUCKER

Harold Shaw Publishers
Wheaton, Illinois

For Corinne and Jack,
our through-it-all friends

ISBN 0-87788-482-X

Cover and interior design by David LaPlaca

03   02   01   00   99   98

10   9   8   7   6   5   4   3   2   1

CONTENTS

WEEK FOUR: FAIRY-TALE LOVE

WEEK FIVE: SEX 'N STUFF

WEEK SIX: THE STRESS MESS

WEEK SEVEN: GROWING PAINS

WEEK EIGHT: DON'T ASK ME TO WALK ON WATER

CHECK IT OUT!

Don't let anyone fool you. Growing up is tough. Whether it's big things, like your parents getting a divorce, or something little, like getting a zit on your nose before your first date with Mr. or Ms. Wonderful, there will always be something that bugs you. It takes a lot of guts and determination to hang in there.

But you know what? You aren't alone. And you aren't weird. Lots of other teens feel the same way.

Maybe your family is a real pain (who says living with your family is a piece of cake?), or you feel rotten about the way you look in the morning (it gives new meaning to the word *scary)*, or maybe you want to be one of the guys, and they leave you out. Perhaps you're head-over-stomach in love with a guy, and he definitely doesn't feel the same way. Or maybe you went "too far" on your last date, and you feel guilty.

Life is filled with rough stuff. In one day, you are presented with millions of little or big crises—what to wear, whether to sneak that first drink with the guys at lunch, how to act around the popular kids, whether to tell your best friend that you're pregnant, choosing a college. And you can think of many more.

In these pages, you'll find stories about teens like you and your friends, space to scribble in, and things to think or pray about during the rest of the day. When life is a hassle, turn to this book. And there's a bonus: you'll get to know God, the Master Problem-Solver, better too!

Jeff and Ramona Tucker

WEEK ONE
FAMILY HOT SPOTS

DAY ONE
LOVE TO HATE MY FAMILY

Wear your sweater, dear. It's cold tonight, you know," her mother advised. Kari gritted her teeth. Mom *always* treated her like a baby in front of her friends, and it was really embarrassing.

"Yeah, um-hum," Kari muttered and whisked out the door with Angelo, her date (and without her sweater).

"And don't forget to be home by ten tonite. You need your sleep, too!" her mother called after her.

Gimme a break, Kari thought. *I'm not a baby anymore.* Slightly red faced, she avoided looking Angelo in the eye the rest of the night. She was in the depths of despair.

MY BROTHER'S A DRAG AND MOM'S A NAG

Being treated like a baby probably isn't the only thing that bugs you. Maybe your mom is trying to make you into a perfect human being ("Make your bed," "Do your homework," "Do the dishes," and "Get straight A's") or your dad won't let you listen to rock, even Christian rock, because he says it's evil. Or maybe your brother gets on your nerves because he's always in your space, bugging you to do something with him. Or your sister digs through your clothes, finds your secret diary, and broadcasts it to the guy you're in love with. But you know what? You can't get reassigned. Your family is all yours—even if you hate to love 'em.

LIFE WITH YOUR FAMILY

> Children, obey your parents in the Lord, for this is right.
> *Ephesians 6:1*

Ouch! That hurts! You don't always want to obey your parents, especially when you are angry. But growing up means not only growing in independence and making decisions on your own but also consulting with your parents instead of yelling at them. If you ask questions and prepare to listen, you'll be surprised what you'll learn. Someone in your family may think of a solution you never could have thought of on your own!

Ephesians 6 doesn't just tell you what you should do; it goes on to tell you *why* you should do it:

> "Honor your father and mother"—which is the first commandment with a promise—"that it may go well with you and that you may enjoy long life on the earth."
> *Ephesians 6:2-3*

What a terrific promise! The rewards are great!

LET IT OUT

Which person in your family do you have the most problems with? Write down his/her name here: _____
(And then go lock this book in a safe place!) Why does that person bug you?

_____

_____

The next time that person rubs you the wrong way, set up a time to talk it out together.

But wait: before you talk, ask God to help you show that person how much you love him/her. If you go with open ears and a loving heart, chances are that you'll learn a lot about yourself and your brother, sister, or parent. You might even discover that you love to like 'em! Working and growing together is what God's family is all about.

DAY TWO
MAD AT DAD

That STINKS!" roared Kevin, racing upstairs to his room and slamming the door. Just because he'd been fifteen minutes later than their agreed-upon curfew last Saturday, he was grounded. Dad wouldn't let him go out with the guys this weekend.

Kevin groaned and punched his pillow. *Of all the weekends, why this one?* This was the big weekend—the end-of-the-school-year class trip—and every one of the guys would be there. Except for him.

Dad was such a stick-in-the-mud sometimes. Kevin really got sick of it. Sometimes he wondered if his dad enjoyed punishing him or something. It was like a power game between him and his dad every weekend. If he got lower than a C in any class, he was grounded for a whole week. And Dad always stuck to the rules like glue. *Just this once, I wish he'd give in and let me go,* Kevin thought. But he knew it wouldn't happen. Dad rarely budged on his decisions.

Kevin flipped the dial on his radio until he found the loudest, rowdiest rock song. Then he turned it up—full volume. *That'll show him,* Kevin thought. *He can't get the best of me!*

BUG OFF!

Parents. *Aargh.* Everyone says that they're a gift—you're not so sure. Sometimes you wish you didn't have any. You're tired of having to hang up on your favorite buddy just because your phone hours are over. And if you hear, "Is your homework done?" one more time, you think you'll throw up.

Maybe, like Kevin, you wonder what would happen if they gave in—just once—and let you do something you wanted to do.

PARENTS NEVER LET YOU DO NOTHIN'

Feeling ticked off at parents is nothing new. Sometimes parents are unfair—surprise! You know why? They're human, just like you. They don't have eyes in the back of their head to prove that your sister Suzy started the fight, not you. And maybe when you get a bad grade, they feel frustrated because they know you could do better—and want you to do better. You've heard the phrase: "If they didn't love you, they wouldn't punish you," right? Well, it's true. God has given your parents the special joy of helping to mold you into who you'll become (for good or bad). And that's the purpose of discipline—to make you a loving, understanding person who will be a gift back to God.

After King David had slept with Bathsheba (another man's wife), God punished him. But God also gave him a hug afterward and brought joy back into his life. Listen to David's words:

> Create in me a pure heart, O God,
>   and renew a steadfast spirit within me.
> Do not cast me from your presence
>   or take your Holy Spirit from me.
> Restore to me the joy of your salvation
>   and grant me a willing spirit, to sustain me.
>   *Psalm 51:10-12*

And that's just what God will do!

PARENT PACT

When do you get mad at your parents? And why?

_____

_____

The next time you're mad at one of your parents (or both), sit down with them and make out a contract like the following one so that you'll both know what's going to happen if a trust is broken:

> I _____ *(your name)* agree that _____ *(you fill in the task or curfew hour or whatever the problem is and what you plan to do about it).*
>
> If I break this contract by _____ *(being late, yelling at my sister, getting a bad grade, etc.),* then you'll discipline me by _____ *(fill in the form of discipline—grounding, extra chores, etc.).*
>
> Signed,
>
> _____   _____   _____
> *(your name)*   *(parent/s' name)*   *(date)*

You know what? The more you work together with your parents, the less you'll probably have to use the contract. And you may discover that your parents can turn it into a privilege contract:

> Since you, _____ *(your name),* have followed _____ *(name of task, agreement)* faithfully, we have decided to give you this: _____
> *(for example, a half-hour later curfew on weekends).*

Be creative!

DAY THREE
NOT A BRADY BUNCH FAMILY

That's it! I've had it with you. You expect me to starch your shirts, iron your stupid ties, and basically be your house slave! Well, I have a life, too, you know!" Mom screamed.

"What's your problem?" Dad yelled. "I ask you to starch one lousy shirt, and you explode!"

"Well, if you . . ." Mom retorted. And the battle raged on.

Lena shuddered. Ever since she could remember, Mom and Dad had been fighting. She got so sick of it sometimes she actually wished they'd get divorced. They were always threatening it anyway. And then she felt guilty for even thinking that.

Somehow her night out with Mike had lost its appeal. *I don't want to turn out like Mom and Dad, and I just know I will! So why bother going out?* Lena thought. *I'll just make a mess of things like they have.* She hurried to the den and called Mike to cancel their date.

SATURDAY NIGHT'S MAIN EVENT

Do you ever feel like your parents don't love each other anymore? (Or at least you could never guess by the way they throw words around every Saturday night.) Or maybe you know your parents really don't love each other because they're getting a divorce. You feel like the smushy middle part of an Oreo—stuck between two hard crusts.

There are many reasons why parents fight—job pressures, personality differences, misunderstandings about roles at home (maybe your mom expects your dad to mow the grass and he hates it!), time pressures, a too-crowded schedule.

SHOWDOWN

What bugs you the most when your parents fight?

_____

_____

When your parents fight, don't take it personally. It's not your fault—even when your dad uses you as a Ping-Pong ball against your mom. Your parents have made choices about how to live their lives and how to relate to each other.

Maybe, like Lena, you feel uncomfortable with dating—you don't want to end up just like Mom and Dad. But you aren't a computerized mini-version of them, programmed to make the same mistakes. You have choices about how you will build relationships. You need others, and others need you (see Hebrews 10:24-25). If you start building your relationships on appreciation, responsibility, courtesy, and honesty, you'll go a long way toward having a peaceful home—a house that's filled with God and his kind of love.

HOME SCENE

When you feel discouraged at home, remember this verse:

In you, O LORD, I have taken refuge;
let me never be put to shame;
deliver me in your righteousness.
Turn your ear to me,
come quickly to my rescue;
be my rock of refuge,
a strong fortress to save me.
Psalm 31:1-2

Today when you go outside, pick up a small rock and put it in your pocket as a reminder of God's solid-as-a-rock love.

DAY FOUR
PLAYING THE PART

H ey, Paula," Tami asked, "Are you okay?"
Paula stirred the ice in her coke. "Yeah, I guess . . . well, no.
"What's going on?"

"It's rotten at home—with Dad gone. Mom doesn't even act like my mom anymore. Sometimes, I feel like I have to mother my brothers because she can't handle it. You know, stuff like cooking and cleaning. She doesn't even want to go shopping anymore. And I can't talk to her about my problems, or she starts crying about Dad's being gone!"

Tami sighed. Poor Paula. The bottom had dropped out of her world six months ago when her dad walked out on her mom and the family. Tami reached over and hugged Paula. She didn't know what else to do to make her feel better.

YOU'RE NOT ALONE

You probably know at least one young person who lives in a single-parent home. Maybe it's you. When parents separate or divorce, it's pretty rough on the kids. Suddenly, your parent can't help you work on your car or teach you to cook. You feel lost, like part of you is missing. And it is.

But you know what? Being a single parent isn't easy either. Can you imagine being Mom and Dad, holding down a full-time job to make ends meet, then coming home to be cook, chauffeur, encourager, attender of all activities—to mention a few? You'd have to be in two or three places at once! That's how many single parents feel—torn between the things they need to do and want to do.

FLIP SIDE

Did you know your attitude is contagious? If you're always complaining that your dad can't cook like Mom did, your dad may feel like a failure. And if you tell Mom she's a loser because she can't tell one wrench from another, she may burst into tears.

The key to all families is communication. If you feel bummed about one parent leaving, talk about it with your other parent. Tell Mom or Dad that you're upset and explain the reasons why. Your parent may be struggling with the same feelings—maybe like Paula's mom, your mother feels worthless and useless since your dad left. She doesn't know if she can be a mom anymore. But if you work together, you'll find that you can *still* be a family—and maybe even a closer one!

BEING A BUD

Write down the name of a teen who is struggling with a single-parent home:

_____

If it's you, decide now to share with your mom or dad this week how you're feeling. Make some notes here:

_____

_____

When you feel uncertain about your family life, God can encourage you through these verses:

> This is the confidence we have in approaching God: that if we ask anything according to his will, he hears us. And if we know that he hears us—whatever we ask—we know that we have what we asked of him.
> *1 John 5:14-15*

If your friend is hurting, ask him or her out this week for a Coke or to come over to your house. Be creative. Find a way to take him or her aside and ask, "How's it really going?" Then listen—with all ears. But don't stop there. Promise your friend that you'll pray for him or her. Then keep your promise.

DAY FIVE
THE STEPPARENT SCENE

Toby toyed with his spaghetti, wrapping it around his fork. *Tomorrow is the big day,* he thought. He tried to swallow the big lump in his throat. *She's really gonna do it.*

Yep. Mom was getting remarried tomorrow. It wasn't as if Toby minded—after all, Jack was a great guy and he really liked him. But what about Dad? Toby had always hoped that someday Mom and Dad would hit it off again, and they could be a family.

But that wasn't all that was bugging him. He wondered how Dad would take it. Toby still loved his dad, in spite of everything. And yet, Mom had been happier in the last year than he could ever remember her—even when Dad was around.

GIMME A BREAK

You can't blame Toby. Big changes don't happen easily. And it's probably hard enough just watching his mom date. After all, dating is for teens, right? Old people can't date—that's downright silly. And getting remarried—to someone else—impossible. In Toby's mind, his mom doesn't belong with anyone but his dad.

Adding someone new to your home is a challenge—it doesn't matter whether it's a new parent or a new baby. Things *will* change. But you don't have to be afraid of change:

> Do not be anxious about anything, but in everything, by prayer and petition, with thanksgiving, present your requests to God. And the peace of God, which transcends all understanding,

will guard your hearts and your minds in Christ Jesus.
Philippians 4:6-7

Some wonderful things can happen. Just wait and see!

GIVING IT A GO

If you (or someone you know) have a parent who's getting remarried, go out of your way to spend a little extra time with your parent's new (or soon-to-be) partner. Ask your mom or dad questions so you'll know what to talk about. Above all, be unselfish (and we know it's hard in this situation!). Don't just think of yourself—realize your parent is searching for happiness too. So try to be happy for your parent.

I'M GETTING A NEW . . .

If your parent is getting remarried, list the negative things about Mom or Dad getting married again (having to adjust to a new person, new rules):

_____

_____

Now jot down the positive things (laughter in the house again, extra money to go to Disneyland or to the movies):

_____

_____

Life with a new parent won't always be easy, but God can help you have a good attitude toward your parent and his or her new partner.

WEEK TWO

NOBODY LIKES ME

DAY ONE
COOL TO BE CRUEL

Hey, TEN TON. What size do you wear now?" Al walked down the hall, ignoring the catcalls that erupted on either side of him.

He didn't mind the nickname as much as the laughter. That killed him. *Maybe someday I'll have a friend—just one—who doesn't care how I look.*

But as he rounded the corner into Mr. Beanham's math class, he wondered. People had never taken an interest in him—so why should they start now? He was doomed to be alone forever.

DIAL AN INSULT
Big Al. His name is right beside the word *lard* in the dictionary. At seventeen, he's never been out on a date. He hasn't even dared to ask a girl—he knows she'd say no or that he'd embarrass her for life if he asked her. His classmates have done a pretty good job of smashing his ego over the years.

Who doesn't snicker at a good putdown? How often have you called someone *Pizza Face, Geek, Idiot, Thunder Thighs, Loser, or Dork?* It's funny—at the time. At least until you're the one receiving the putdown.

OUCH!
Words do hurt. Why do people put others down? For many reasons: to get attention, to fit into a certain group, or to feel good about themselves. With so many people tearing others down, teens desperately need positive peers. In Romans, Paul reminds us: "Try to build

each other up" (Romans 14:19, NLT). Colossians tells us that we are representatives of Christ in everything that we say and do. Before you open your mouth, think of this verse:

> Therefore, as God's chosen people, holy and dearly loved, clothe yourselves with compassion, kindness, humility, gentleness and patience. Bear with each other and forgive whatever grievances you may have against one another. Forgive as the Lord forgave you. And over all these virtues put on love, which binds them all together in perfect unity.
> *Colossians 3:12-14*

STICKS AND STONES . . .

Listen to a few conversations on your next school day. How many of them build people up? How many tear people down?

_____

_____

How many times did you make a nasty comment about someone else today? Be honest. What did you say (or think)?

_____

_____

The Bible says if we *think* something bad, it's just as bad as if we actually *did* it (see Matthew 5:28).

How can you be a positive peer this week?

_____

_____

Who is the person everyone makes fun of in your school? The next time your friend rags on him or her, decide what you will say. And then stick to it! God will stand proudly by your side.

DAY TWO
ZITS ON DATE NIGHT

Nicole squinted into the mirror and winced. *Aargh! Not today!* There they were—two nasty, puffy-looking zits—on her chin. And right before senior prom too.

"Gross!" she exclaimed and caked on the Clearasil. Of all the days for her skin to act up, it had to be the morning before her first date with Mr. Perfect—Brian Barker, the football captain.

After covering her face in three coats of makeup, she grabbed her schoolbag and dashed out the door.

I just hope no one notices, she thought. But inside she knew those zits were as big and bright as traffic lights.

IS THAT REALLY ME?
Who doesn't look in the mirror in the morning and wince? Maybe, like Nicole, you think your adolescence is erupting all over your face. Or maybe you just feel fat and downright ugly. Or you think your looks are as interesting as a piece of blank paper.

Looks aren't everything. Yeah, you've heard that before, but you really don't believe it. After all, Suzy Gorgeous gets everything—cheerleader, homecoming queen, and all the dates she wants just because she has fluffy blonde hair and tan skin.

IT'S A DOWNHILL BATTLE
You know Suzy's gorgeous body? Well, it won't look so gorgeous when she's fifty. In the long run, it doesn't matter what you *look* like, but *who* you are—inside, underneath your clothes, hairstyle, and the facade you put on. God cares more about your heart:

The LORD doesn't make decisions the way you do! People judge by outward appearance, but the LORD looks at a person's thoughts and intentions.

1 Samuel 16:7, NLT

Isn't it neat to know that there's one VERY BIG person who just cares about the real you?

SELF-CHECK

Write down words to describe yourself (or draw a picture of yourself):

_____

_____

Then ask a friend to do the same for you. Jot down your friend's comments.

_____

_____

Compare the two lists. Bet you're surprised!

When you're down in the dumps about yourself, read over 1 Samuel 16:7 and also your friend's list. You are valuable to your friends and to God!

DAY THREE
QUIRKY QUIRKS

Hey, sweet stuff! Whatcha' doin' tonight?" Rob's voice rang loud and obnoxious against the lockered hallway.

Julie sighed. "Get lost, Rob," she answered.

"Let's go to a movie," he said (yelled). "I heard *Return of the Nerds* is great."

Yeah, and you belong in it, Julie thought.

"I wanna go with you," Rob whined. "After all, we're buddies, right?" And right there, in front of all her friends, he put his sweaty, hairy arm around her.

Julie thought she was going to gag. Today she didn't feel like being a Christian.

HOW HUGGY IS TOO HUGGY?

Rob is a huggy guy. He turns other kids off. What Julie doesn't know is *why* Rob is that way, and she doesn't really care to find out.

Maybe you feel the same way. You want to punch your "Rob" out every time he treads too close to your turf. Or maybe you are Rob, and you don't know what to do about it.

"I JUST WANNA BE LOVED"

Many times boisterous people think they have to be loud in order to get attention. Just like everyone else, they want to be liked—to be one of the group. Inside, they don't feel anyone really likes them, so they have to be pushy. And because they're pushy, people bad-mouth them and mistreat them. It's a nasty circle. No one likes to be caught in it.

If you struggle with being kind to "loud" people, this verse is just for you:

> Live in harmony with one another. Do not be proud, but be willing to associate with people of low position [people you don't like]. Do not be conceited.
> *Romans 12:16*

And if you're one of the "loud" people, keep the following verses in mind:

> Do not repay anyone evil for evil. Be careful to do what is right in the eyes of everybody. If it is possible, as far as it depends on you, live at peace with everyone. Do not take revenge, my friends, but leave room for God's wrath, for it is written: "It is mine to avenge; I will repay," says the Lord.
> *Romans 12:17-19*

In other words, you shouldn't take out all your bad treatment on others!

ICKY ME

List the things you don't like about yourself:

_____

_____

Which ones are possible to change? Map out a strategy for attacking the things you *can* change. Ask God to give you the courage to carry out your plan and to encourage you when you need it.

Oh, one more thing. A smile goes a long way in making friends. Try it—it works!

DAY FOUR
FRIDAY LATE, WITHOUT A DATE

It was Friday night—again. Ann sat in front of the TV in her usual spot, with the bowl of popcorn on her lap. She had the *TV Guide* memorized. After all, there was nothing else to do.

Ann lives in a small town that has a bad case of the normals. Everything about it is boring—no Dairy Queen, no youth group at her church. Sure, kids from school got together, but they didn't invite her. Why should they? She's always pretty quiet around groups and no one really knows her.

Well, I really wouldn't have wanted to go anyway, she lied to herself, sinking further into the pillowy couch.

SCARED SOCKLESS, BORED MINDLESS

Are you like Ann? Do you sometimes feel bored out of your mind because there's nothing to do or nobody to do something with?

Maybe, like Ann, you're shy around the kids at school and don't let them get to know you. Or else you're okay with just one person, but going out with a group of kids scares you. So you take the easy route and withdraw.

NOT ALWAYS A MERRY-GO-ROUND

It really doesn't matter whether you're by yourself or in a large group—you can still feel lonely. But did you know that loneliness is a choice? *Your* choice?

Life is not an amusement park of constant, fun rides. It has a lot of ups and downs. And it's up to you what you do with them.

NO MORE MR. OR MS. COUCH POTATO

If you don't have friends, take some initiative. Write down the name of one person you'll call this week and invite to do something with you (go out for ice cream, play tennis at the park, etc.).

_____

Here's a hint: If you're chicken to try it out on the kids at school first, try your brother or sister (or a parent).

Look for ways to help other people out. Maybe there's an older lady down the street who needs her house dusted or help getting groceries. Or you could help your younger brother with his homework.

List two people that you could help out in the next month, and what you could do for them:

_____

_____

Then carry out your plans! God tells us that serving others brings joy and purpose into our lives:

> If you have any encouragement from being united with Christ, if any comfort from his love, if any fellowship with the Spirit, if any tenderness and compassion, then make my joy complete by being like-minded, having the same love, being one in spirit and purpose. Do nothing out of selfish ambition or vain conceit, but in humility consider others better than yourselves. Each of you should look not only to your own interests, but also to the interests of others.
> *Philippians 2:1-4*

When you are busy helping others, you'll never be bored. Pray and ask God to give you busy hands and a helping heart.

DAY FIVE
FREE TO BE ME

Arnie walked off the basketball court and slouched down on the bench. He just knew Coach was out to get him. Sure, it was his fault for screwing up on his lay-up in the last big game, but he didn't deserve to be treated like this. Everyone acted like he was the biggest loser in town.

"Your brother wouldn't have messed up that lay-up," Coach had yelled. The words still gnawed at Arnie's self-image.

I'm not as great as my brother—so what? Arnie steamed on the bench. *I'm me—and nobody seems to care about that.*

He was humiliated.

HIGH EXPECTATIONS

No matter who you are, someone has high expectations of you—your parents, a brother or sister, a school teacher, a Sunday school leader . . . the list is enormous. When you don't match up, then you feel like a loser. Maybe you got a C in geography (you can't even find the United States on a map) and your parents hit the roof—*they* always got A's in high school. Or your dad is upset because you're too scrawny to play football—he was the fullback on his high-school varsity team.

THE PRESSURE'S ON

Who puts pressure on you? (Mom, Dad, teachers, yourself?) To do or to be what?

How does it make you feel?

_____

_____

TURNING DOWN THE HEAT

You aren't just like anyone else, and you have value. You know who said so? Someone who knows—God. He's known you even before your parents did. Jeremiah 1:5 says: "Before you were born I set you apart [and] appointed you." God created you for a special purpose, and he wants you to be free to be the person he made you to be. The apostle Paul, someone who knew God well, says:

> And we know that in all things God works for the good of those who love him, who have been called according to his purpose.
> *Romans 8:28*

Wow! That means God has something just for you to do, and nobody else can do it like you can. Ask God to help you define yourself in *his* eyes.

WEEK THREE

MY FRIENDS SAY I SHOULD . . .

DAY ONE
GANGBUSTERS

It was eleven o'clock in the south side of Chicago. Mitch glanced down the street, checked his watch, and then walked quickly to the corner store. Just before he reached the door, he pulled on a black ski mask and fished a revolver out of his pocket. He flung the door open and yelled, "Hand it over—all of it!"

As he raced out the door and toward the War Lords' headquarters, he couldn't believe how easy it had been. All those scared, stupid people had let him take all their money. For the first time in his life, someone feared him. It gave Mitch a charge. His gang initiation was over. He knew he'd look great in the War Lords' leather jacket.

ONE OF THE GANG

Mitch wants what everybody else does—to be popular, to feel accepted by a group, to be "one of the guys." But there's a problem—he isn't picking the right set of friends. They want him to steal to prove his loyalty. And Mitch is so into the War Lords that he isn't thinking about what might happen to him if he gets caught.

How many times have you done things just because someone else did them or expected you to do them? Maybe you stole something, cheated on a test, or even gave drugs a try just because all of your friends were watching.

CLIQUES AND CLONES

Popularity is a nasty word. Why? Because determining whether you are "popular" or not means you're going by what someone else thinks of you—not by who you really are.

When you want friends, don't look for the most popular clique or gang in your school. Keep your eyes open and watch for teens who share your same values and concerns. Before you get involved with a group, ask yourself these questions:

- What's the purpose of the group?
- Does the group encourage you to do bad things (like lying, drinking, stealing, smashing windows, etc.)?
- What kind of a reputation does the group have?
- Does this group help or hurt other people?
- How will being in this group affect your future?

CROWD-BREAKER

It's really true that who you are with affects who you become. As one very wise man who had been through a lot (the apostle Paul) said:

> Don't be misled. . . . You will always reap what you sow! Those who live only to satisfy their own sinful desires will harvest the consequences of decay and death. But those who live to please the Spirit will harvest everlasting life from the Spirit. So don't get tired of doing what is good. Don't get discouraged and give up, for we will reap a harvest of blessing at the appropriate time. Whenever we have the opportunity, we should do good to everyone, especially to our Christian brothers and sisters.
> *Galatians 6:7-10, NLT*

If you could make yourself from scratch, what type of person would you want to be? Scribble down your ideas.

_____

_____

Today when someone pressures you, follow Jesus, not the crowd.

DAY TWO
SAYING YES TO NO!

J ust a sec." Debbi scowled at her little brother and covered the mouthpiece on the phone. "Get lost, you little brat!" she yelled, and he scampered outside.

Debbi turned her attention back to the phone. She couldn't believe Andrea and the other popular junior girls were actually asking her to go along to a big party. Of course, she knew that it wasn't chaperoned (she could just see explaining that to her mom and dad) and that everybody would be drinking, but she couldn't say no. Could she? They'd probably never ask again.

"Yeah, sure. I'll come," she stuttered. "Friday night? . . . great . . . no, don't come here. I'll—uh—meet you guys." As she hung up, fireworks of excitement exploded in her brain.

But as she got ready for bed, she couldn't avoid the nagging doubt that she should have said no.

A GOOD PUT DOWN

Debbi is a Christian. But she doesn't want to be known as an old fuddy-duddy who won't do anything fun—just because she's a Christian.

All of us are sometimes tempted to be ashamed of who we are and what we stand for. After all, who wants to be teased? Or worse—avoided?

FIRMING UP YOUR NO

It's hard to say no. But here are some ideas that may help:

- Decide ahead of time what you want to do if you are asked to go somewhere you don't really want to go.
- Be friendly to the person, but firm. Let your no be NO.
- When all else fails, appeal to rules and possible consequences.

God gives you some added muscle power for saying *no:*

> Remember that the temptations that come into your life are no different from what others experience. And God is faithful. He will keep the temptation from becoming so strong that you can't stand up against it. When you are tempted, he will show you a way out so that you will not give in to it.
>
> *1 Corinthians 10:13, NLT*

Just think: every time you're tempted to do something wrong, there are thousands of other teens who are also tempted! But God says he'll always give you a way out. Thank him in advance for the help he's going to give you and ask him to remind you of his promise in 1 Corinthians 10:13 when the going gets tough.

"NO" POWER

When have you found it hard to say no? To what people? In what situations?

_____

_____

What are some alternate activities you could suggest?

_____

_____

The next time people push you to do something wrong, suggest one of the alternate activities. You may be surprised when they think it sounds like fun!

DAY THREE
NOT OF THIS WORLD

Randy cringed. This looked like a weird place.

"Come on, Randy. Let's go inside," Drew said excitedly. "There's all sorts of cool stuff in here. I've been here before."

Reluctantly Randy followed him in. It didn't look like a normal store. Everything was dark and—well—eerie. Randy felt the way he did last year on Halloween night when someone sneaked up behind him and scared him.

"Hey, take a look at this thing," Drew called. "It's a Ouija board—you can get messages from dead people and stuff like that."

Randy shivered, but still he was curious. The guys in his gym class talked about stuff like this. After all, it was just a piece of wood. Nothing to it. What could it hurt?

HEEBIE-JEEBIES

Talking to dead people. Looking for ghosts and things that go bump in the night. Sound creepy? It is. With all the horror movies that are out, maybe those kinds of things don't freak you out anymore. They seem routine. Kids at your school play with Ouija boards at parties. It's no big deal, you think.

But it is. The spirit world is very real—it's nothing like white-sheeted ghosts on Halloween night. Satan is just waiting to drag you into his territory and give you the worst fright of your life. But he's sneaky. He doesn't scare you with the big stuff until he's hooked your curiosity in the little things—like reading your horoscope every day.

That's what happened to Marcy. First, she got into bands with scary lyrics; then a friend invited her to a seance, and pretty soon she was buying *The Satanic Bible.* Now she can't sleep at night because she hears terrifying voices.

What makes Satan worship so fascinating? Satan offers what you want most—power and pleasure. He'll give you all the sexual thrills, drugs, and revenge you want. That sounds pretty good if you feel powerless and unaccepted, or if you want revenge on someone who has treated you badly. Satan wants you to believe there are no limits—you can do whatever you want to do, and indulging yourself will fill the emptiness inside.

But that's a big fat LIE—Satan's best trick. You know what Satan's agenda for your life really is? John 10:10 tells us: "The thief [Satan] comes only to steal and kill and destroy." He wants to ruin you.

What about God? Take a look at God's agenda in the same verse: "I have come that [you] may have life, and have it to the full" (John 10:10).

What a difference—Satan offers *death,* but Jesus offers *life.*

DEVILISH DABBLING

Messing around with the occult or with Satan worship isn't a game. It's *warfare.*

> For our struggle is not against flesh and blood, but against the rulers, against the authorities, against the powers of this dark world and against the spiritual forces of evil in the heavenly realms.
> *Ephesians 6:12*

God has some harsh words for those who dabble even a little bit in the spirit world: "If we claim to have fellowship with him yet walk in darkness, we lie and do not live by the truth" (1 John 1:6). He also says that no one can be partly his and partly the devil's. You're one or the other.

For you were once darkness, but now you are light in the Lord. Live as children of light (for the fruit of the light consists in all goodness, righteousness and truth) and find out what pleases the Lord. Have nothing to do with the fruitless deeds of darkness, but rather expose them.
Ephesians 5:8-11

Who are you going to belong to?

HATE, LIES, AND ALIBIS

How can you tell if a friend is getting involved with Satan? Here are some things to watch for: involvement with an Ouija board, a fascination with horror films and music about death and violence, collecting Satanic symbols and literature, always acting hateful and vengeful. If your friend is interested in the spirit world (Satanism, witchcraft, whatever), what good reasons can you give him or her for discontinuing that practice? Make some notes here.

_____

_____

Ask God to help you talk to your friend without getting drawn into what he/she is doing. (It would be a good idea to talk with a parent or a youth leader and get their support. They may want to come with you and talk with your friend.)

Faithfully pray for your friends, asking Jesus to

... open their eyes and turn them from darkness to light, and from the power of Satan to God, so that they may receive forgiveness of sins and a place among those who are sanctified by faith in [God].
Acts 26:18

Christ is the only one who can snatch someone who's been involved with Satan out of darkness into light.

44

DAY FOUR
SMOKING IN THE BOYS' ROOM

Hey, somebody's coming!" the guard at the door whispered.

Tom sucked a last long drag and then threw his cigarette into the john and flushed it.

To Tom, lunch hour was the only good thing about school. He hated studying, and classes were boring. School had been an absolute yawn until he made friends. When his friends were smoking, it didn't seem so wrong. So he tried it and liked the way it made him feel more cool and relaxed. Then several months ago at a party he'd discovered beer. Suddenly he didn't feel inhibited anymore. He could party like everyone else.

WHERE DO I BELONG?

What is Tom really looking for? A place where he'll be accepted for just who he is. The only problem is that he's looking in the wrong place. His "friends" don't want him to be himself; they want him to be part of the group.

What about you? Have you ever felt pressured to drink at a party? The funny thing about parties is that the other kids feel uncomfortable if you don't drink because then you're not like everyone else. It's easier to be part of the crowd—and to think as a crowd—than to stick up for what you believe in.

BOMBED OUT OF YOUR MIND

You probably know that alcohol and drugs are contributing factors in most fatal traffic accidents, suicide attempts, and murders. Most likely, you've heard that until you choked on it (it's the standard parent speech to make you not want to drink or smoke pot).

But maybe you haven't thought about this: When you're bombed out of your mind, there's no telling what you might do or have done to you. Two months after a party at a friend's house Tanya discovered she was pregnant—and she couldn't even remember having sex because she was drunk!

Here's another good reason for not doing drugs and alcohol: the apostle Paul says that your body is a temple of the Holy Spirit:

> I plead with you to give your bodies to God. Let them be a living and holy sacrifice—the kind he will accept. When you think of what he has done for you, is this too much to ask? Don't copy the behavior and customs of this world, but let God transform you into a new person by changing the way you think. Then you will know what God wants you to do, and you will know how good and pleasing and perfect his will really is.
>
> *Romans 12:1-2*, NLT

If you're a Christian, Christ lives in you. That means if you put junk into your body, you are putting junk in Christ's body.

GARBAGE IN, GARBAGE OUT

Make a "What Goes In" list of all the junky things you put into your body. They don't have to be cigarettes or beer; they could be things like eating junk food constantly instead of healthy food, reading sleazy magazines, going to R-rated movies, playing trashy computer games. Make another list of "What Comes Out"—a bad attitude, a headache from too much TV, unhealthy relationships.

_____   _____

_____   _____

_____   _____

_____   _____

God can help you "fix" the junky things you put into your body. Ask him for the power to help you toss them into the garbage where they belong and leave them there—permanently.

DAY FIVE
THE MAKE-OUT QUEEN

Every time Joanna walked down the hall at Fremont High, people whispered, "There she goes. The Make-out Queen. Did you hear about? . . . " Then they would launch into a juicy piece of gossip.

Joanna didn't care anymore. She was past that. She'd made a big mistake a year ago in "going all the way" with Paul Brandt—Macho Mouth—and she was branded for life. It wasn't like any of the other girls didn't make-out—they just didn't get caught.

When Joanna first came to Fremont last year, she was lonely. Everyone seemed to run in cliques, and she didn't belong anywhere, until she met Paul, that is. But she didn't know what he was after. On the second date, she found out—sex. But Joanna didn't really mind; someone finally liked her and cared about her.

Then Paul had dumped her flat. Joanna felt used. She wasn't a virgin anymore, so why not sleep around if she found someone she liked? It didn't matter anyway.

MAKING LOVE

How many times have you heard that phrase? If you're not married, "making love" is just that—*making* love, trying to create the *feeling* of closeness with sex. Physically it feels good, but emotionally it's like putting ice cream around a Brussels sprout. You taste the sweet stuff and don't realize you're swallowing something nasty until the ice cream's all gone.

Don't let anyone deceive you about sex. It's a great thing in the right context. But "making love" with someone won't make that person love you or want to continue to date you.

WHY NOT?

Because God wants you to be free of the physical burdens of premarital sex: possible pregnancy, sexually transmitted diseases, AIDS, and the constant longing to have more once you've had sex. He wants you to be free from the emotional burdens, too: the possibility of breaking up (did you know that many couples who have premarital sex break up because of the pressure?), loss of your virginity (which you would have liked to save for that one special person on your wedding night), the ties and regrets. And spiritually, sinning destroys your relationship with God. When you sin, most likely you feel like running away from God and hiding (Adam and Eve did!).

In order to protect us, God gave us these words:

> Run away from sexual sin! No other sin so clearly affects the body as this one does. For sexual immorality is a sin against your own body. Or don't you know that your body is the temple of the Holy Spirit, who lives in you and was given to you by God? You do not belong to yourself, for God bought you with a high price. So you must honor God with your body.
> *1 Corinthians 6:18-20,* NLT

What a value God places on you!

NEVER TOO LATE

If you have a friend who's sexually active, what can you tell him or her to keep him or her from sleeping around?

_____

_____

If you have been or are sexually active, it's not too late for you. Your past doesn't have to rule your future. God is wonderfully loving and forgiving. He's ready to forgive you, to hear you say you're sorry and that you're ready to make some changes. Ask him to help you when you feel pressured by your boyfriend or girlfriend or anyone else.

And ask someone you know to hold you accountable—a close friend or an adult you feel comfortable with. You may also want to try group dates for a while until you get stronger. And above all, avoid alone places where you feel tempted to slip back into your old habit.

God says, "Don't be afraid, for I am with you. Do not be dismayed, for I am your God. I will strengthen you. I will help you. I will uphold you with my victorious right hand" (Isaiah 41:10, NLT). With God's help, you can stay pure—or become pure again.

WEEK FOUR
FAIRY-TALE LOVE

DAY ONE
IT'S THE REAL THING

Jennifer melted back against her locker, a starry look in her eyes. "Isn't he just *adorable?*"

Lisa rolled her eyes and smirked. This time Jennifer was in love with Kent, all because he'd said hi to her in the hallway. Last week Marty got Jennifer's attention.

Lisa shook her head, "You're a case, Jen. I never knew anyone who switched guys so much."

Jennifer stared dreamily down the hall. "But Lisa, he's the one. I just know it."

Ha! Lisa thought. *I've heard this before!*

LOVE OR INFATUATION?

I'm in love. How many times have you heard—or said—that? Chances are you've been in love at least two times in one school year. Or is it infatuation?

Sometimes it's hard to tell the difference when emotions are running high. But there's a way to tell if your love is the real thing. Check it out against this:

> Love is patient, love is kind. It does not envy, it does not boast, it is not proud. It is not rude, it is not self-seeking, it is not easily angered, it keeps no record of wrongs.
>
> *1 Corinthians 13:4-5*

A TALL ORDER

Whoa! Wait a second! That means if you're really "in love" with someone, you'll never get mad at him (or her), or snub him if he snubs you, or keep track of who does dirt to whom and when. Paul goes on:

> Love does not delight in evil but rejoices with the truth. It always protects, always trusts, always hopes, always perseveres. Love never fails.
> *1 Corinthians 13:6-7*

What a tall order! But that's God's definition of mature love.

I LOVE YOU, I THINK

If you are interested in someone or are dating someone, here are some questions you should ask yourself. Jot down your answers.

Do I like the way my boyfriend/girlfriend acts? Am I proud of him/her? How do I treat him/her?

_____

_____

Could I live with him/her for the rest of my life—bad habits and all? How does he/she treat me?

_____

_____

How does your relationship stack up against 1 Corinthians 13:4?

_____

_____

When you pray today, ask God to help you make the right decisions about whom to date (or not to date).

DAY TWO
IN LOVE WITH LOVE

Michael slammed his locker and sprinted out the door. He wanted to be alone.

What's wrong with me anyway? he wondered. *Am I ugly or something?* He just knew Charlotte was the girl for him. He had been in love with her since sixth grade, and finally, four years later, he had enough guts to ask her out.

She'd said no. *No!* he exploded. *How could she say no? I've been nice to her all my life.*

That night he was so angry at God that he couldn't even pray. His life was ruined. If God wouldn't make Charlotte go out with him, then he'd get even with God. *Forget praying,* he fumed. *You don't help me anyway, God. So why should I bother?*

THE COLD SHOULDER
Poor Michael. How many times have you been "in love" with someone who didn't quite feel the same way about you? Pretty painful, huh? You start wondering if you're ugly, or overweight, or if you need a new tube of Clearasil, or if your wardrobe needs overhauling. *Of course it can't be me,* you reason. *Why would anybody want to pass me up?* But, mysteriously, they do. And it hurts. Especially if you have your heart set on having a boyfriend or girlfriend.

PRIORITY THINKING
You want to know something amazing? Believe it or not, if God wants you to have a boyfriend or girlfriend, he will give you one without your trying to force him. God always wants you to be the

best you can be. That may mean a special relationship—or it may not.

Many times you don't know what's best for you (whether you want to admit it or not). But God does, even when you don't understand what he's doing. As Isaiah said:

> "For my thoughts are not your thoughts,
>   neither are your ways my ways," declares the LORD.
> "As the heavens are higher than the earth,
>   so are my ways higher than your ways
>   and my thoughts than your thoughts."
> *Isaiah 55:8-9*

God is concerned about you. He wants you to get your priorities straight (something hard to do when you are ga-ga over that gorgeous guy or the girl with the model figure). God wants you to realize that no matter what, he has to come first in your life.

SOMEONE SPECIAL FOR YOU

If you don't have a boyfriend/girlfriend, how do you feel about that?

_____

_____

If you do have a special someone, how are you doing priority wise? How can you focus your attention more on God? Do you take time to listen and talk with him—even when you're dating someone? Why or why not? Make some honest notes here.

_____

_____

DAY THREE
BLACK & WHITE

Chad couldn't believe his parents could be so bigoted.

Trista was a great girl and belonged to his youth group at church. But that didn't seem to matter to Chad's mom and dad because Trista was black and Chad was white.

What's the big deal, anyway? Chad wondered. *God created us all equal, right?* Besides, the last thing he wanted to do was tell a nice girl like Trista he couldn't go out with her just because she was a different color. He didn't care if she was black, purple, or green—he liked her personality.

DAZED AND CONFUSED

How many times have you been interested in somebody, and your parents have put the kabosh on it for some reason? Or maybe you haven't even tried to do anything about your interest because you know your parents wouldn't go for it.

GRAY AREA

So what about interracial dating? Is it okay or not? The Bible says that we're all created equal. Take a look at this:

> So you are all children of God through faith in Christ Jesus. And all who have been united with Christ in baptism have been made like him. There is no longer Jew or Gentile, slave or free, male or female. For you are all Christians—you are one in Christ Jesus.
>
> *Galatians 3:26-28, NLT*

In the Old Testament, God was against races marrying other races—but it was for religious reasons, never racial reasons (see Ezra 9:1-2 and 10:1-2). God didn't want the Jews to marry nonbelievers. So race and culture doesn't divide the family of God, but faith does. If you're interested in dating someone of another race, first make sure that other person is a Christian.

Here's something else to think about: Dating sometimes leads to marriage. Biblically there's nothing wrong with marrying a person of another race (as long as both of you are Christians). But if things are getting serious, keep your future in mind: you'll most likely have to live in an area where mixed-race marriages are accepted. It will be easier for the two of you than it will be for your kids (many biracial children get teased mercilessly by other children). Your eyes may be full of stars, but there's lots to think about!

GOD'S RAINBOW OF PEOPLE

How do you treat teens of a different race than you?

_____

_____

How do you feel about dating a guy or girl of a different race?

_____

_____

No matter how you feel about dating other races, if your parents are dead set against it, you'd be wise to date teens of your own race. It will make for a much calmer home all-round, and you'll be following God's command to obey your parents.

If you're struggling with whether to date someone, ask God to show you a well-rounded picture of that person, and get some advice from an adult you trust. If you discover that you hold prejudices against people of a different race, ask God to help you to be open-minded and loving.

DAY FOUR
THE YOKE'S ON YOU

Come on, Jack. You never want to do anything anymore. What's wrong with you?" Emily asked.

Jack wondered that himself. When he'd started dating Emily five months ago, he couldn't think of anything or anyone else. But lately, he'd sensed that something was missing in their relationship. They really didn't have that much in common, and he was getting drawn into doing a lot of stuff he didn't want to do.

Yeah, come to think of it, I haven't even been to youth group in five months. Emily didn't want to go—she ignored anything religious. But she was so much fun, and Jack was sure he really loved her. What should he do?

FIT TO BE TIED

Jack is trapped. He's trying to go one direction, and his girlfriend's trying to go another. Now that the initial fun of dating is over, he's discovering that the relationship isn't all he wants it to be. "Love" can be blind sometimes!

Let's say you meet this fabulously awesome hunk of a guy, or a cute girl who's—well—just *perfect*. The only problem is that your "perfect" person isn't a Christian. So what should you do? Here's what the Bible says about it:

> Do not be yoked together with unbelievers. For what do right-
> eousness and wickedness have in common? Or what fellow-
> ship can light have with darkness? . . . What does a believer

have in common with an unbeliever? *2 Corinthians 6:14-15*

Wait a minute, you're saying. *That's talking about* marriage, *not* dating, *right? I'm not planning on marrying this person.* Frankly, the Bible doesn't say there's anything wrong with having non-Christian friends, but trouble comes when you begin to date a non-Christian. It's a greater attachment. Love is too easy to start and too hard to stop. Opening yourself to falling in love with someone God doesn't want you to marry can lead to pain and frustration for both of you. And it can draw you away from God.

BACK ON TRACK

Are you dating a non-Christian? Or do you know someone who is? Write down the reasons why you—or your friend—shouldn't, from God's perspective (you may want to reread 2 Corinthians 6:14-15):

_____

_____

If you're dating a non-Christian, ask God for courage to break off your relationship. Don't use "missionary dating" (dating someone to help him or her become a Christian) as an excuse. Ask God to help you get back on the right track spiritually. And then take comfort in these words of love:

> In you, O LORD, I have taken refuge;
> let me never be put to shame.
> Rescue me and deliver me in your righteousness;
> turn your ear to me and save me.
> Be my rock of refuge,
> to which I can always go.
> *Psalm 71:1-3*

If you aren't dating someone now, ask God to help you keep his priorities in mind when you get interested in someone. God is the only One who can be a refuge day and night, forever.

DAY FIVE
ROSES AREN'T ALWAYS RED

Natalie stared at the ringing phone. She didn't even want to answer it. She knew it would be Craig.

Seven months ago, dating Craig was every girl's dream. But the dream had been turning into a nightmare. Craig insisted that Natalie be with him when *he* wanted her; other times he would blow her off. Lately, all he wanted to do was make out.

Natalie put her face down on her arms and sank onto the kitchen table. She couldn't stand the pressure anymore—she just wanted to be rid of him, and he wouldn't leave her alone. She wished she were a heavyweight champ and could knock him out—*POW!*—forever.

BREAKING UP IS HARD TO DO

Okay. This guy you dated ONCE keeps following you around the school halls. You want to get rid of him. Or maybe the guy you're dating is a lot slower paced than you, and it drives you crazy. Or maybe you're scared of your boyfriend—like Natalie—and wish you could break up with him. You're afraid that if you do, he'll hurt you (he may be abusing you already). Whatever the case, it's hard to get rid of people once there has been a dating relationship.

HARMFUL OR HELPFUL?

When should you break up with somebody? If there is:

- emotional abuse (telling you that you're no good, that no one else would want you)
- physical abuse (your boyfriend/ girlfriend grabs your arm and bruises it, hits you, or forces you to go all the way sexually)
- spiritual mismatch (only one of you is a Christian)
- different life goals (one of you wants to become a bartender and the other a missionary)
- overemphasis on making out (that's all you do)
- no joy or trust and you can't be yourself

THAT'S THE END, FOLKS

How should you break up? If you aren't dating someone you need to break things off with, you probably have a friend who does. Share this section with your friend.

First, write down your reasons and motives for breaking up (this will help when you get flustered in talking to your boyfriend/girlfriend).

_____

_____

Ask close friends to help you go over your reasons and also to pray with you. Read these verses to give you courage:

> If you need wisdom—if you want to know what God wants you to do—ask him, and he will gladly tell you. He will not resent your asking. But when you ask him, be sure that you really expect him to answer, for a doubtful mind is as unsettled as a wave of the sea that is driven and tossed by the wind.
> _James 1:5-6, NLT_

When you talk with your boyfriend/girlfriend, be definite about saying, "I won't be going out with you anymore." Leave no room for "if's" and "maybe's." Tell the truth in love and then claim victory over your dating situation with these words: "In all these things we are more than conquerors through him who loved us" (Romans 8:37).

Afterward, you may feel sad. And you may even miss that relationship at times. Don't worry—these emotions are normal. They don't mean you made a bad decision. So give yourself a break—and some time to heal.

WEEK FIVE
SEX 'N STUFF

DAY ONE
MR. HANDS

Alicia sat stiffly in the far right side of her chair. This guy was too much! It was only their second date, and he acted like he owned her. She hadn't really minded the old stretch-yawn-and-just-happen-to-put-your-arm-around-the-girl ploy—much. But when he started caressing her knee during the second hour of the movie, she'd had enough!

Alicia decided that this was her last date for a long time, maybe forever. She was sick of handsy guys.

GUYS WHO CLING LIKE TIGHT SWEATERS
Maybe you've gone on a "mercy date" (you felt sorry for the guy) and he touched you on the shoulder or brushed up against you—on purpose—all night. You knew you were going to throw up as soon as you got home. Or a guy in class (a real geek) is always coming up to you and hugging you, and you can't stand it.

Guess what? Guys aren't the only ones who can be "handsy" on dates. Girls can be pretty aggressive, too! One girl we know likes to feel guys' muscles and purposefully trips so a guy will help her up.

PROPERTY LINE
The touching game. It goes on all the time. But your body is *your* property—and God's—and no one else has the right to touch any area without your okay.

Touching a girl or guy may feel great, if you really like that person. God has made our bodies to respond sexually in a thrill of delight when we're touched. That's the way he prepares us for marriage and a wonderful life with one partner. But God gives a stern warning about that:

> Marriage should be honored by all, and the marriage bed kept pure, for God will judge the adulterer and all the sexually immoral.
> *Hebrews 13:4*

The only problem during dating is that the God-designed thrill feature makes you want to do more—it's only frustrating. So playing the touching game doesn't do either of you any good.

TOUCHY FEELY

How are you doing on playing the touching game? Do you think you have to kiss your date good night just because it's a date? Why or why not?

_____

_____

It's smart to decide ahead of time what you will and will not do. Here's a good rule to remember: *Don't do anything on a date that you'd be ashamed of telling your future husband or wife.*

Before you go out on a date, read this psalm. It'll encourage you to stand up for what is right.

> How can a young person stay pure?
> By obeying your word and following its rules.
> I have tried my best to find you—
> don't let me wander from your commands.
> I have hidden your word in my heart,
> that I might not sin against you.
> *Psalm 119:9-11, NLT*

DAY TWO
THE BACK-SEAT GUILT TRIP

Mark sat up in the back seat of his Buick and buttoned his shirt. He was disgusted with himself. He didn't know what came over him around Lori—maybe it was her perfume. Going out with Lori without wanting to be alone was just impossible. And of course, being alone always led to more.

Mark's mind was swimming, bogged down with his conscience. Well, he and Lori *did* love each other. So was making out so bad, if they maybe, kinda, sort of were planning on getting married next year after high school?

WHAT A FOX!
Mark's logic is working overtime to get himself out of being the bad guy in this situation. Chances are that Mark and Lori *won't* get married. It's not Mark's logic talking; it's his hormones.

Have you ever drooled over a good-looking guy? Or whistled at a cute girl? Did you know that the Bible says it's just as bad to look at a guy or girl and think "sex" as it is to make out with him or her (Matthew 5:28)?

HELP FOR HORMONES
You know you shouldn't get involved sexually. You've heard the old parental speech: "You might get pregnant and ruin your life." But how can you make your thoughts stick when your hormones are racing? Ask yourself some questions in advance:

- Is the relationship growing (do you have a friendship)?
- Do you communicate well (not just sexually)?
- Do you spend all your time alone or are others a part of your relationship?

The answers to these questions will show you how mature and healthy your relationship is.

God leaves no place for sexual intercourse in dating—not because he's a die-hard party-pooper, but because he loves us and knows that premarital sex leads down a dead-end road.

> Be imitators of God, therefore, as dearly loved children and live a life of love, just as Christ loved us and gave himself up for us as a fragrant offering and sacrifice to God.
>
> But among you there must not be even a hint of sexual immorality, or of any kind of impurity, or of greed, because these are improper for God's holy people. . . . For of this you can be sure: No immoral, impure or greedy person—such a [person] is an idolater—has any inheritance in the kingdom of Christ and of God.
> *Ephesians 5:1-3, 5*

DRAWING THE LINE

Before you go out, agree with your date on limits. How far is too far? Do you know why to resist sex? Are both of you tough enough not to let things get out of hand? Be honest.

Make careful plans in advance of what you're going to do: go shopping, to a movie, or out with a group of friends for ice cream. List some fun ideas.

_____

_____

If you've already gone too far, it's not too late for you. God can make you a virgin again in your heart and mind:

If we confess our sins to him, he is faithful and just to forgive us and to cleanse us from every wrong.

1 John 1:9, NLT

So move on. Philippians 3:13-14 says, "Forgetting what is behind and straining toward what is ahead, I press on toward the goal to win the prize for which God has called me heavenward in Christ Jesus."

God is waiting to forgive you for your past and to give you a new reason for living. Why not write out a prayer to him right now?

_____

_____

DAY THREE
MISUSED & ABUSED

The neon light of her clock said 2:00 A.M. Cristina couldn't sleep. She kept thinking about what had happened.

Terrence is my friend, she wept. *How could he have done that to me?*

She and Terrence had gone to a movie and then for a walk through the park. He made a move to kiss her, and she flinched—after all, it was their first real date. But then he grabbed her arm, hard, and kissed her anyway.

"Come on, baby, don't be such a prude," he said. And even when she resisted, he'd unbuttoned her shirt. Cristina had been paralyzed. *This kind of stuff only happens in movies,* she thought.

"Terrence, lay off!" she said. But he forced her down on the ground, under the park trees, and made her do the big "it." Then he picked himself up off her, told her to get dressed, and took her home.

Cristina was shaking and scared. She didn't ever want to see Terrence again, and she didn't want anyone to find out why.

CRIME OF VIOLENCE
Cristina is mixed up. You can't blame her. She thought she was going out with a nice guy, and he *forced* her to have sex.

Whether Cristina knows it or not, she's been raped. Rape doesn't happen just with strangers who jump girls in dark alleys. Reports show that at least half of the women (or men) who get raped *know* the person who raped them.

So what's the difference between making out and date rape? *Sex without consent is rape*—there's no way around it. And, guys, it can happen to you, too.

How does it start? Usually, your date will try to talk you into having sex; then he or she may start to get physical. How can you protect yourself? There's no foolproof method, but these things may help:

- As soon as your date starts getting handsy, set sexual limits (it's your body and God's—you have the right).
- Trust your feelings (your gut will tell you if something isn't right).
- Pay attention to rough and unwanted behavior (your date pushes you or begins unbuttoning your shirt).
- Above all, be assertive and stand up for yourself. Get out of the car (or house) immediately if you sense something isn't right.

Remember that you can always call on God in times of trouble. Write these verses on a card and carry it with you until you have them memorized:

The LORD is my rock, my fortress and my deliverer;
  my God is my rock, in whom I take refuge.
  He is my shield and the horn of my salvation, my stronghold.
I call to the LORD, who is worthy of praise,
  and I am saved from my enemies.
  Psalm 18:2-3

God is our refuge and strength, an ever-present help in trouble.
  Psalm 46:1

HOW TO GET HELP

If you or someone you know has been date raped, she may have a hard time talking about it. She may be afraid, have a hard time trusting guys, or have nightmares. She may wonder when the guy is coming back to get her and if it's her fault. (A lot of people lay blame on the person who gets raped—"it's the way she was dressed." This is not true; rape is a crime of violence, not of passion.) She also may wonder if the guy will tell stories about her. So talking it out with someone like you is important.

But don't try to handle what's happened by yourself either. You or your friend should talk to a counselor, a church youth leader, or your local police immediately. Ask God to help you be a sensitive friend this week, and also to help you make wise decisions about the person you date.

DAY FOUR
SHAUNA'S SECRET

Shauna stared at the ceiling and wondered if she could run away—and get away with it. The last time she'd tried, her father had caught her sneaking out the door with her bag and had whipped her with a belt. Shauna just couldn't handle the sound of her father's footsteps anymore, or the smell of him when he came toward her bed, or the pain she felt when he made her have sex.

Everyone thought she had the perfect family; how could she talk about what was *really* going on? Her friends would be shocked if they knew. Just once she wanted to be a normal kid in a normal family.

SOMETHING'S GOING ON, BUT NOBODY'S TALKING

Sexual abuse. It goes on every day—not only among criminals but among husbands and wives, among fathers and daughters, mothers and sons, fathers and sons, stepfathers and stepdaughters, brothers and sisters (incest), and among people who date (date rape).

Most of the time when it happens in the family or between friends, it goes unreported. Like Shauna, the person may think it would be too embarrassing, or that it would break the family apart. Underneath, the person may worry that what happened is his or her fault.

WHO'S TO BLAME?

But the abused person is the *victim;* the abuse is never his or her fault. People who sexually abuse others are mentally sick. They need help, or the abuse will continue.

In Old Testament days, Tamar was abused by her half-brother, Amnon. He wanted her body and he wanted it bad. So he took it—without her permission. He committed incest. But he didn't get off scot-free: when Tamar's real brother Absalom found out, he had Amnon killed (see 2 Samuel 13:28-29).

God has a heavy-handed slam for sexual abusers:

> No one is to approach any close relative to have sexual relations.
> *Leviticus 18:6*

In God's eyes, there is no gray area about sexual abuse. It's plain WRONG. The person who abuses God's law will be punished.

WHERE CAN YOU TURN?

Do you have a friend who has been abused, or have you been abused? It may not be sexual abuse, but physical or emotional. Write down what has happened or is happening and how you feel about it in a private notebook.

Is there a person you feel comfortable talking to—a friend, church youth leader, guidance counselor, a parent? Ask God to give you the guts you need to talk with that person RIGHT AWAY about what is going on.

Put this verse by your bed so that when you're bothered with bad dreams, it'll be handy:

> The LORD says, "I will rescue those who love me.
>   I will protect those who trust in my name.
> When they call on me, I will answer;
>   I will be with them in trouble."
> *Psalm 91:14-15, NLT*

If you are experiencing abuse, remember: *It's not your fault.* God doesn't blame you, and you shouldn't blame yourself. But you need to speak up so you will get the help you need, so the person who abused you will get help, and so that person will not abuse you again. For immediate help, call the national child abuse hotline at 1-800-421-0353.

DAY FIVE
AM I WEIRD?

J eremy watched Jenna walk down the hall, swinging her hips.
What's wrong with me? he wondered. *Don't I have hormones or something?* All the guys thought Jenna was the hottest girl alive—they got turned on just watching her.

Jenna didn't do anything for Jeremy. In fact, no girl did. Sometimes he wondered if he was gay or something.

THE BIG LIE
It seems like everyone today is talking about sexual preferences and rights. Movie stars and politicians are "coming out." The Gay Rights people say it's okay, that being gay is being normal. After all, if a guy wants to sleep with a guy, or a girl with a girl, it's his or her choice, right?

GOD'S VIEW
God says something different. Take a look at 1 Corinthians 6:9:

> Do you not know that the wicked will not inherit the kingdom of God? Do not be deceived: Neither the sexually immoral nor idolaters nor adulterers nor male prostitutes nor homosexual offenders nor thieves nor the greedy nor drunkards nor slanderers nor swindlers will inherit the kingdom of God.

If you want more ammunition, read Romans 1:18-27. God says that any sexual intercourse for anybody outside of marriage is wrong. *But wait a minute,* you're thinking, *some homosexuals and lesbians now are getting married.* But same-sex marriage is definitely not God's plan.

Check out Genesis 2 for one very obvious reason: part of the plan of marriage was to create children—just try that naturally with a same-sex marriage! God designed sex for male and female.

THE RIGHT KIND OF CHOICES

God does give us choices, but he expects us to make them within the framework of his Word, the Bible. If you wonder if you're gay, don't despair. You do have a choice—your questions about your sexuality don't have to control you or your behavior. God can help you stay pure and not act on your feelings.

If you know someone who's wrestling with these feelings, how do you treat that person? Does anyone at your school have AIDS? Are you one of the kids who says behind his or her back, "Look at that gay guy or lesbian?" Do you just ignore that person? People who choose to be homosexual in their sexual lifestyles are sinners like everyone else; they should be treated with compassion.

If you or a friend is struggling with the *Am I gay?* question, or with having AIDS, you can ask God for help and forgiveness. Remember though: God is not a "gimme" God. Saying you're sorry for your behavior doesn't mean that God will automatically wipe out the consequences of your sin, like AIDS or herpes. But he'll never leave you or forsake you. God's love is forever:

> For I am convinced that neither death nor life, neither angels nor demons, neither the present nor the future, nor any powers, neither height nor depth, nor anything else in all creation, will be able to separate us from the love of God that is in Christ Jesus our Lord.
> *Romans 8:38-39*

When you're struggling with questions about sexuality, go to an adult you trust and be honest about your thoughts and feelings. And remember, too, that when you feel weak, God has a firm grip on you. He can help you!

WEEK SIX
THE STRESS MESS

DAY ONE
WHEN PUSH COMES TO SHOVE

Get out!" yelled Thor. "And don't EVER come back!" He shoved his little brother out of his bedroom.

Kid brothers! A-a-a-rgh! I never get any time—or room—to myself, Thor thought. He was feeling quite sorry for himself.

Thor knew he shouldn't have yelled at his brother—or pushed him for that matter. Ever since Dad had lost his job two months ago, Thor's whole family had been tense. Mom had to get a job to help out with the bills, and even Thor had been chipping in on groceries—out of his *own* part-time job after school.

Now it seemed like Dad didn't want to go back to work. He just sat around and watched TV all day, ignoring the family. Thor was plain disgusted. Sometimes he wanted to march right up to Dad and shove him off that old couch.

But deep down inside Thor was more scared than ticked off. Dad wasn't acting like Dad anymore.

STRESSED OUT

Thor is majorly stressed out right now. How can he look up to his dad when his dad is acting more like a kid than a father? There have been some intense changes in Thor's life.

Maybe your dad hasn't lost his job. But maybe you, like Thor, are feeling stressed out. Not only are you the "Perfect Kid" at home but you're V.P. of student government, and you're on the basketball team. Everyone expects you to be #1 at everything. Or maybe you live with a single parent and feel like you have more chores to do than other kids your age.

BATTLING THE BUMMERS

Stress. We all cope with it differently. Thor's first reaction was to get angry—he threw his kid brother out of the room (well, you know how little brothers are—maybe the kid was asking for it). When you feel stressed, you may get angry, or you may withdraw in silence. Sometimes you can't sleep. You're afraid you'll mess up your Super Achiever record so your stomach ties itself in knots.

Life will always be stressful. But whatever happens (losing first chair flute in band, not making varsity football, flunking a test) can't hurt you. Only your *reactions* to what happens can. If you're snotty to the girl who made cheerleader instead of you, you're only hurting yourself. You'll become angry and bitter, and no one will want to be around you.

A WAY TO COPE

But God doesn't leave you to handle life all on your own. He gives you comfort in lots of different ways. In his Word, he promises he'll help you in times of stress:

> Then they cried to the LORD in their trouble,
>   and he saved them from their distress.
> He brought them out of darkness and the deepest gloom
>   and broke away their chains.
> Let them give thanks to the LORD for his unfailing love
>   and his wonderful deeds.
>   *Psalm 107:13-15*

God may also surprise you with a special friend (your own age or older) with whom you can share your up and down times. God may lead you to a wonderful place where you feel loved and protected (like a youth group) and where people pray for you.

When do you feel most stressed out? Why?

_____

_____

What do you do when you feel stressed (yell at the dog, beat your pillow, cry)?

_____

_____

Scribble down some ideas for how the stress you're under could help you to grow closer to God and others, and to learn more about yourself.

_____

_____

Above all, remember that God will help you when push comes to shove. He's the ultimate Stress Protector!

DAY TWO
YOU'RE WHAT?

Karen's hands shook as she hung up the phone. *I can't believe this is really happening!* she agonized.

She should have known better. The last month she'd been really sleepy at school and had felt nauseated all the time. But she never dreamed that she might be pregnant!

How could she tell Jon? Sure, they knew that getting pregnant was a possibility when they fooled around, but she never thought it would happen to her. How could she tell her friends? Everyone thought she was such a "good girl."

THE PG WORD

Karen isn't the only one. More teens than ever today are becoming pregnant before they reach the age of eighteen. We're sure you know at least one girl in your high school who was or is pregnant. (What you don't know is how many more have had abortions secretly.)

Hearing about AIDS and herpes and other such stuff isn't enough to scare some people away from having sex. Like Karen, you may think it could never happen to you, so if it feels good, you do it. You'll get away with it, right?

A GAME YOU CAN'T WIN

But that's not what God says. He makes it pretty clear that when we sin, we get burned. Proverbs warns us against having sex outside of marriage:

> Can a man scoop fire into his lap without his clothes being

burned? Can a man walk on hot coals without his feet being scorched?

Proverbs 6:27-28

When we sin, we always can ask God for forgiveness (which he gives readily). But all the "I'm sorry's" in the world won't change the result of sin. Karen is still pregnant.

WHEN YOU BLOW IT

If Karen were your friend, what would you say to her? Write down some ideas here:

_____

_____

(Remember that your place is not to judge her. You could be in her place someday—but we hope not!)

If you or a friend are pregnant, the first thing God wants you to do is to ask his forgiveness. Something simple like: "God, I'm really sorry. I blew it. It was my fault. Help me to deal with this baby's coming even if I'm not happy about it."

When you or your friend are discouraged about the baby or the comments that other teens make, read this:

But as for me, I watch in hope for the LORD,
   I wait for God my Savior; my God will hear me. . . .
Though I sit in darkness,
   the LORD will be my light.
Because I have sinned against him,
   I will bear the LORD's wrath,
   until he pleads my case
   and establishes my right.
He will bring me out into the light;
   I will see his righteousness.
   Micah 7:7-9

DAY THREE
DEALING WITH "IT"

Remember Karen from yesterday? She was really scared to tell her parents that she was pregnant. They had big plans for her: college, then law school. And Jon—they'd only been dating four months. The last thing Jon would want to be—at seventeen—was a *father.* She was scared of losing him.

Maybe I should just get rid of the baby, Karen agonized. *Then no one would ever have to know.* After school she checked out an abortion clinic that she'd heard other girls from school talk about. The lady who talked to her there was nice and everything, but she kept calling it Karen's "problem" and the baby an "IT." Karen didn't know what to do.

ABORTION

Getting rid of the problem seems so easy. Sure—one simple operation and IT's gone. For good. Then life can return to "normal," you think, and no one will ever know. All those things sound pretty good to someone who's just found out that she's pregnant.

But there's another side to the issue. What the pro-choice (pro-abortion) lady at the clinic didn't tell Karen is that the IT is actually a baby, already imprinted with God's image. Check out this verse from Genesis, the story of creation:

> So God created man in his own image,
> in the image of God he created him;
> male and female he created them.
> *Genesis 1:27*

GOD KNOWS YOU

God knows every child—even when the child is just being formed in the mother's womb:

> For you created my inmost being;
>> you knit me together in my mother's womb. . . .
> My frame was not hidden from you
>> when I was made in the secret place.
> When I was woven together in the depths of the earth,
>> your eyes saw my unformed body.
> All the days ordained for me
>> were written in your book
>> before one of them came to be.
> *Psalm 139:13, 15-16*

Every baby who's conceived is stamped with the image of God. Job says, "For the life of every living thing is in his hand, and the breath of all humanity" (12:10, NLT). Destroying that creation is, in one simple word, *murder.* Having an abortion doesn't help you get rid of the "problem" or your sin; it adds murder to it.

There's also the emotional and physical side. Many pregnant teens who have abortions have a hard time having babies later in their lives because the operation has made them sterile. Most teens feel a great emotional burden of shame and guilt when they discover that the IT they've killed was actually a baby. Their quick, fix-it solution—abortion—becomes a lifetime burden.

THERE'S MORE TO IT

If you or a friend are pregnant, how do you feel about the baby?

_____

_____

Write down your reasons (or help your friend write down her reasons) for having an abortion, and then jot down reasons for not having an abortion.

Having Abortion   Not Having Abortion

_____   _____

_____   _____

Take a look at the reasons for having an abortion. How many of them are selfish? Be honest.

If you want to discuss your pregnancy with someone who doesn't know you, call 1-800-B-E-T-H-A-N-Y for free crisis counseling (open from 8:00 A.M.–12:00 midnight). They're good listeners!

If you or a friend has already had an abortion, you may feel like a bad person. You wonder if God will ever forgive you for what you did. But did you know that in God's eyes, *none* of us is good, that we're all murderers in our hearts? Although God doesn't count all sins equal (killing a person versus stealing a candy bar), he forgives all of them equally. Don't let your shame and guilt hang over you for a lifetime. Ask Jesus today for his forgiveness . . . and wait for his shower of love!

DAY FOUR
ADOPTION OPTION

Karen slumped in her hospital bed and touched her flattened belly. Some months ago she'd agreed to give her baby up for adoption, but now she wondered if she was doing the right thing. Andrew was a part of her. How could she give him up?

But there were no other choices. She had no money, her parents were dead set against her keeping the baby, and Jon didn't want to marry her. Besides, she had to finish high school. What else could she do?

STICKIN' IT OUT
You've got to give Karen credit—she decided not to have an abortion, and she stuck through months of curious and condemning looks from her classmates. When she made the decision to give her baby up for adoption, she knew it was the right thing. But when it finally came down to it, she wasn't sure. Andrew was a part of her, and she would never see him again.

WHY ADOPTION?
When Rosa first found out she was pregnant, she thought about her boyfriend. *Of course Pedro will marry me, as soon as he knows I'm pregnant.* But she didn't stop to ask herself these questions:

- Do I love Pedro? Enough to make a marriage work?
- Will we be able to support a child? (Making a list of how much a baby costs—furniture, diapers, medical bills—will help you or your friend be more realistic.)

- What about finishing high school?
- Would we be the best parents for this child?

These questions bring hard reality to the question of adoption.

THINKIN' IT OUT

Sometimes it's easier to think things out on paper. If you or a friend is considering adoption, make two lists: "What I Can Offer My Child" and "What an Adoptive Couple Can Offer My Child." (You can scribble here or make your own list.)

_____   _____

_____   _____

_____   _____

Now compare the two. Ask God to help you be unselfish in the decision of whether to keep your baby or not. Cry out to God and ask him to encourage you. When David was having a hard time in the desert of Judah, he wrote these words:

> Because you are my help,
>   I sing in the shadow of your wings.
> My soul clings to you;
>   your right hand upholds me.
>   *Psalm 63:7-8*

If you ask him, God will hold you just as he held David.

If a friend has recently given up a baby for adoption, don't think, *Phew! Now that that's over, we can go back to normal.* It's not over for your friend. Sometimes she'll still feel sad and wonder if she's done the right thing. At those times, encourage her to pull out her list on "What an Adoptive Couple Can Offer My Child" and read it over.

DAY FIVE
NO EASY WAY OUT

J ason sat speechless in class. He knew his buddy Jesse had been down a lot lately, but he never dreamed Jesse would try to kill himself! All day he couldn't think of anything else. He kept remembering little statements Jesse had made: "My parents would be better off if I weren't around" and "I'm such a loser." Jason just thought Jesse was bummed and tried to laugh it off. Now he wished he'd listened.

YOU'RE NOT THE ONLY ONE

Have you ever wanted out of life—permanently? That's what Jesse wanted. He couldn't see that his living did any good for anyone— his parents, friends, and, most of all, himself.

If you've ever felt that way, you aren't alone and you aren't weird. Bouncing emotions are normal as your body changes through your teen years. But when you or a friend stays depressed for a long period of time, then it's easy to think of suicide as a way out. It's the old self-pity trip. Come on, count the times you've done it—"Everybody would be better off without me," or "I'm not good at anything."

FINDING A WAY

But God has different ideas. Did you know that even before you were born he called you by name (Isaiah 43:1)? And he chose you—especially—to do something? Take a look at this proof:

> In him we were also chosen, having been predestined according to the plan of him who works out everything in conformity with the purpose of his will, in order that we, who were the

first to hope in Christ, might be for the praise of his glory.
Ephesians 1:11-12

Hey, God planned you! He gave you the number of hours, days, months, and years on earth that he wants you to have—it's his gift. But your time can be your gift back to him. Don't take it away from him. He's excited to see what you're going to do with your life!

TROUBLE ALERT

If your friend is thinking of suicide, you may notice one or more of the following signs:

- talking about death or saying, "Everybody'd be better off if I were dead . . ."
- withdrawing from activities with you and others
- inaction, no enthusiasm for things he/she liked to do before
- sloppiness in dressing or driving too fast
- saying "I'm going to kill myself." (Don't kid yourself that people who talk about suicide don't do it.)

If you want out of life and are considering suicide, reread Ephesians 1:11-12. Christ has *chosen* you—he wants to be the light shining through your dark tunnel (see John 1:1-5). He wants to give you hope and love and understanding. Write this message on a piece of paper and put it where you'll see it throughout the day:

God, you are my light in the darkness, and in you is *life.*

How can you help a friend who's discouraged? Be a good listener. Spend time with your friend; don't always try to cheer her up. Get the person talking—ask him what bothers him the most. But don't push them to talk; they may not be ready to talk.

If your friend is depressed for a long time, talk about seeing a counselor or other trusted adult. Or suggest that he or she make a quick phone call to the Covenant House crisis hotline: 1-800-999-9999.

WEEK SEVEN

GROWING PAINS

DAY ONE
BODY CHECK

Danielle checked out her figure in the mirror and grimaced. She'd give anything to be a size 5 like Pam. She couldn't believe how fat she was—even after all the months of dieting. Even her boyfriend had a smaller waistline than she did. That was pretty embarrassing. After another long look in the mirror, she grabbed her purse and raced downstairs. "No thanks, Mom!" she yelled. "I'll be late if I eat breakfast."

Danielle's mom sighed. She was really getting worried—Danielle had lost ten pounds in three weeks.

MS. VOGUE OR MR. GQ

Let's face it. Everything is a competition for Ms. Vogue or Mr. GQ these days. Just check out a magazine in your grocery store! The models are slim, trim women (they're so perfect they make you sick) and muscled men (who must spend all their time working out and looking in the mirror). And yet, what do we do? Moan and groan and say, "If only I looked like her, or had muscles like him!"

Biologically some people mature faster than others. We know two people who didn't have curves anywhere until college (us—and we think we turned out all right!). But some teens can't handle the pressure. A guy who feels wimpy may withdraw from other guys because he knows he'll never be Mr. Universe. A girl may become anorexic (starve herself) in order to fit into a pair of size 5 Levis. Other girls may become bulimic—eating large amounts of food and then throwing it up in secret.

ALL SHAPES AND SIZES

Did you know that God cares not only about your body but also about you? He doesn't set you beside someone else and play *guess the fatso's weight* or *how many muscles don't you have?* game. He has chosen you for a special purpose:

> But you are a chosen people, a royal priesthood, a holy nation, a people belonging to God, that you may declare the praises of him who called you out of darkness into his wonderful light.
> *1 Peter 2:9*

No matter what you do, God wants you to praise him. Yes, even with your zits and long nose and odd color of hair. He wants you to give thanks for who and what you are! *Yeah, r-i-g-h-t,* you're thinking. *If I have to live with this body, okay . . . but be thankful for it? No way!* But listen:

> Be joyful always; pray continually; give thanks in all circumstances, for this is God's will for you in Christ Jesus.
> *1 Thessalonians 5:16-18*

That means you should give thanks for your body, too!

MIRROR, MIRROR ON THE WALL . . .

How do you feel about the way that you look?

Things I Like   Things I Don't Like

_____   _____

_____   _____

_____   _____

Most likely your list of things you don't like is longer than those that you do!

Now, can you change any of those things? If so, how? (For instance, you can improve your appearance by ironing your clothes instead of pulling them out from under a heap in your bedroom and wearing them.) Jot down some ideas:

_____

_____

Now cross out the things you *can't* change. Write over the top of them these words:

God made me for a purpose and loves me JUST AS I AM!

When you feel bummed about yourself, thank God for making you who you are and ask him to help you be excited about what you and he are going to do today—together!

DAY TWO
REBEL WITHOUT A CAUSE

Marco and Lucius leaned against the door of Radio Shack and watched a red Ferrari whiz by.

"Man, that rich guy's got *everything!* Check out that car!" Marco exclaimed.

"Yeah, and I bet he gets the hot chicks, too," replied Lucius. "He sure doesn't have to steal to get what he wants."

They both sneered, but inside both were thinking, *No one knows what it's like to live in the barrio. Except for us. And our stupid parents who stayed there.*

DO YOU HAVE A B.A.?
Both Marco and Lucius have major B.A.'s (bad attitudes). Because they can't have everything they want, they blame their "bad luck" on everything but themselves: God, their families, their environment. And they use their "bad luck" as an excuse for stealing or fighting with other gangs.

It's easy to think that someone else has it all—good looks, brains, coordination—and that you have nothing. God must have passed you over in the production line or something, so you had to take the leftovers in life.

YOU OWE ME
Do you know people who think the world owes them something?

They don't want to let go of any hurt until they've gotten the mileage out of it. Don't these verses describe Marco and Lucius?

What causes fights and quarrels among you? Don't they come from your desires that battle within you? You want something but don't get it. You kill and covet, but you cannot have what you want. You quarrel and fight. You do not have, because you do not ask God. When you ask, you do not receive, because you ask with wrong motives, that you may spend what you get on your pleasures.
James 4:1-3

God has a different idea. He wants us all to live in peace with each other, not wanting what someone else has:

The wisdom that comes from heaven is first of all pure; then peace-loving, considerate, submissive, full of mercy and good fruit, impartial and sincere. Peacemakers who sow in peace raise a harvest of righteousness.
James 3:17-18

God says that if you do it his way, you'll produce a harvest (an abundance of good things)! Wow!

CHIP ON YOUR SHOULDER

Have you ever been around anyone who seems to be "mad at the world"? (Maybe it's you.) Describe what this person is like.

_____

_____

Find the words in James 3:17-18 that show how we *should* act if we are Christ followers.

_____

_____

When you pray today, ask God to show you how you're doing with the list above. Then circle one word that you want to work on (for instance, *submissive,* if you're having problems dealing with your parents' authority). This week make it a point to act in the way that you *should* act, not the way you *want* to act.

DAY THREE
IT'S NOT FAIR!

Mona, Charles, and Alicia grabbed their books and headed for Dinah's, their favorite after-school spot. "I can't believe it," Mona said softly.

"Yeah . . . he's really dead." Charles absent-mindedly slurped his Coke.

I can't talk about it, Alicia thought. Just yesterday, the four of them had been sitting in this very booth. Now Matt was gone. Last night he'd been thrown off his motorcycle into a telephone pole.

How could God let him die? Alicia wanted to know. But she was too afraid to say anything. After all, she was the "Christian" in this bunch, and they didn't think much of her God to start with.

WHO'S TO BLAME?
Mona, Charles, and Alicia are upset. You can't blame them. Their friend has just been whisked off the face of the earth, and they've been left behind.

When a friend dies, it's easy to get angry at your friend (who was stupid not to wear a motorcycle helmet), at yourself *(Why couldn't I have stopped her from committing suicide?),* or at God *(Where are you anyway, God?).* Maybe the person who died was your best friend, and you wonder if you will ever have a buddy like him or her again. You wonder if anyone else even cares.

LIFE GOES ON
When someone close to you dies, God always notices. He knows about your friend's death and the way you feel about it. Everything

happens in God's time:

> There is a time for everything . . .
> a time to be born and a time to die . . .
> a time to weep and a time to laugh,
> a time to mourn and a time to dance.
>   *Ecclesiastes 3:1-2, 4*

If you and your friend are both Christians, God has promised that death is not the end. You'll see each other again, and be together again, *forever* (Isaiah 26:19). Although this may not make you *feel* happier now, it'll give you a reason to go on, even when you're hurting.

If your friend wasn't a Christian, you may feel terrible—like you failed because you didn't share the good news about Jesus. There's nothing you can do for your friend now, as hard as that may be to accept. Instead of mourning over your friend, ask God to give you the courage to talk to your non-Christian friends about Christ. You can make a difference in their lives.

LIFE AFTER LIFE

Have you ever lost a friend (it could be through moving away, or sickness, or death)? Write about it. How did it feel?

_____

_____

Write down this promise and keep it in your wallet:

> Weeping may remain for a night,
>   but rejoicing comes in the morning.
>   *Psalm 30:5*

If you haven't lost a friend, but know someone who has, make a special point this week to be sensitive to that person. He or she may need extra time to talk over the hurt in a quiet place.

DAY FOUR
K-MART SPECIALS

Hey, kid! Where'd you get those shoes? A garage sale?" the guys in the locker room taunted.

Jared straightened up from tying his laces and joked it off, "Yeah. It was your mom's garage sale, pal!" Joking around was the only way Jared could deal with high school. If he didn't show how much the teasing got to him, maybe they'd quit—eventually. Maybe when he was eight feet tall or something.

Yeah, sure. Jared knew he was a toad. At sixteen, he was four-feet-eleven and eighty-one pounds, dripping wet (once the guys had dragged him out of the shower and weighed him!). Plus, he couldn't wear all the brand-name clothes everybody else did. His parents shopped at Flashy Trashy—for everything.

Great, Jared muttered to himself, *I'm a Grade A, #1 Dork and there's nothing I can do about it.*

THE DORK COMPLEX

Hey, let's face it. Everyone can find *something* they don't like about themselves (you probably have a whole list!).

Maybe cash is tight at your house, and you spend your time moaning about the Gucci purse or Porsche you can't have. Instead you have to drive a rusty brown station wagon, and your purse is a genuine imitation. Or maybe your tight-wad dad cuts your hair (around a bowl) instead of forking over money for a real haircut. Maybe you're short and thin, like Jared, or too wide for your height, and everyone picks on you. Your life is a disaster.

WHAT REALLY MATTERS

Most people see what you look like on the *outside* first, and then judge you on your appearance. But God isn't that way. He cares about your insides. He doesn't want you to be worried about having the right clothes for the right image:

> Therefore I tell you, do not worry about your life, what you will eat or drink; or about your body, what you will wear. Is not life more important than food, and the body more important than clothes? . . . Who of you by worrying can add a single hour to his life? . . . But seek first his kingdom and his righteousness, and all these things will be given to you as well.
> *Matthew 6:25, 27, 33*

If you're following God, he'll supply all your needs: "And my God will meet all your needs according to his glorious riches in Christ Jesus" (Philippians 4:19).

DO UNTO OTHERS . . .

Describe the last time you were teased about the way you look. (We bet you can remember exactly what was said.)

_____

_____

The next time you're ready to cut someone else down, remember how you felt. You're not the only one with feelings!

God wants you to focus on what you *do* have, not what you don't. Make a list of the things you can be thankful for (maybe you're smart at math and can help others, or you have a good relationship with your parents):

_____

_____

Thank God today for at least one item on your list.

DAY FIVE
LIFE'S A SMORGASBORD

With a heavy sigh, Juanita plopped down next to Raul in the library. "How are you doing?" she asked.

"Great, just great," he replied, a bit exasperated. "Man! I can't figure out one college from another! They all blur together after a while."

"Yeah, I know. It's kinda scary . . . deciding your life!" Juanita moaned.

After five more minutes of flipping pages, they decided it was time for an ice cream break.

THIS OR THAT?

Every day you're faced with choices. They can be little or big. Maybe right now *you* are trying to choose a college. You sit there for hours and flip through the wads of flyers in the mail and try to decide: should I go to a university, a technical school, a Christian college? It's like choosing food that you can't identify at a smorgasbord. You have to close your eyes, point, and then grab something.

BUILDING BLOCKS

Every choice you make—even down to choosing cherry pie and Doritos for lunch over soup and a sandwich—makes a difference in your future. How you handle the little choices is a pretty good indication of how you'll handle the big ones. For instance, if you can't stop yourself from snarfing down three chocolate bars at once just because you want them, will you be able to say no to sex on a date? (After all, it might make you "feel good.") Cheating on a test can become a way of life—later, you may steal time from an employer by not working as hard as you should or by taking longer coffee breaks.

The choices you make do indicate value. And with each choice you make comes responsibility and judgment. (By the way, choosing *not* to make a choice is still making a choice!) Some choices aren't black and white—for instance, which college to attend. But others, like deciding not to put someone down, are.

So what do you do when you haven't got the foggiest idea what you should do? *Always, talk to God. Get his help. And then move in small steps.* Did you know that God has plans for your life? Check out what Jeremiah, the prophet, said:

> "For I know the plans I have for you," declares the LORD, "plans to prosper you and not to harm you, plans to give you hope and a future. Then you will call upon me and come and pray to me, and I will listen to you. You will seek me and find me when you seek me with all your heart."
> *Jeremiah 29:11-13*

When you're confused about choices you need to make, remember that God wants to give you hope—and a future! What could be better?

TUG-OF-WAR

What decision or choice do you have to make in the next week? Write down the pros and cons of either side of the choice.

Pros   Cons

_____   _____

_____   _____

_____   _____

Now check out the pros and cons against this passage in Romans:

> Love must be sincere. Hate what is evil; cling to what is good. Be devoted to one another in brotherly love. Honor one another above yourselves. Never be lacking in zeal, but keep your spiritual fervor, serving the Lord. Be joyful in hope, patient in affliction, faithful in prayer. Share with God's people who are in need. Practice hospitality.
>
> Bless those who persecute you; bless and do not curse. Rejoice with those who rejoice; mourn with those who mourn. Live in harmony with one another. Do not be proud, but be willing to associate with people of low position. Do not be conceited.
>
> Do not repay anyone evil for evil. Be careful to do what is right in the eyes of everybody. If it is possible, as far as it depends on you, live at peace with everyone.
>
> *Romans 12:9-18*

Whether your choice is little (deciding to talk with the new girl in school) or big (telling a gossipy story that would hurt someone's reputation), these verses will help to put it into the "eternal" perspective. Ask God to help you develop an eternal perspective when you have to make choices.

WEEK EIGHT

DON'T ASK ME TO WALK ON WATER

DAY ONE
POPULARITY CONTEST

Fred stuffed his chemistry notebook in his locker and slammed the door. Just then he heard shuffling behind him. Oh no! It was Tyrone and his cronies.

"Hey, Father Fred. So whatcha doin' this weekend? Readin' your big fat Bible?" Tyrone taunted.

Fred felt sick. Last year when he was a new Christian, he'd brought his Bible to school so he could tell everybody about Christ. He'd never been able to live it down. Now everyone called him "Father Fred," or "Bible banger."

Sometimes Fred wanted to throw all this Christian business out the window. He wanted to be popular—just once.

CASHING IT IN?

How many times have you felt like cashing in your Christianity? If you're a Christian and other kids at your school know about it, you probably get hassled, too. (And if you go to a Christian school, teens are still divided into the "in-crowd" and the "rebels" so you're not immune, either.)

BLUE RIBBONS

Surprise! There is no first-place prize for being Mr. or Miss Popular. You won't find it in a trophy case or stamped on anyone's T-shirt, because it doesn't last for long.

Take a poll at your school. Who were the "popular" kids last year? List their names.

_____

_____

Now list who the "popular" kids are this year.

_____

_____

Most of the time these lists will be very different. Popularity goes in and out, depending on whether on not you make cheerleader, or varsity football, or the lead in the play.

But there's one kind of popularity that won't change and that's the way God feels about you. He's promised you a far greater prize than popularity could ever bring you:

> Jesus said to [the disciples]: "I tell you the truth, at the renewal of all things, when the Son of Man sits on his glorious throne, you who have followed me will also sit on twelve thrones, judging the twelve tribes of Israel. And everyone who has left houses or brothers or sisters or father or mother or children or fields for my sake will receive a hundred times as much and will inherit eternal life. But many who are first will be last, and many who are last will be first."
> *Matthew 19:28-30*

We'd much rather be first forever than first for a year, wouldn't you? God's kind of popularity is forever.

GOD'S POPULARITY SCALE
Think of the reasons you admire the popular kids. Are these characteristics temporary—popularity for a day, or year—or eternal? Ask God to give you wisdom and strength to care about what really matters in the long run.

DAY TWO
THE DOUBT BOUT

Wednesday night was Bible study night. But Valerie didn't want to go ever again because God had taken her little sister away.

What kind of God are you anyway? she'd yelled, when she'd found out Katrina had leukemia. And through all the months she'd watched Katrina suffer and then, finally, die, she'd grown angrier at God.

Now she wondered if her sister's death had been her fault. She hadn't always been very nice to Katrina, even before she got sick. *Did you take her away because I was mean to her?* she'd asked God several times.

But she never seemed to get an answer. Now she was convinced that all this Christian stuff was a scam—and she was mad at herself for falling for it all these years.

DOUBTING THOMAS

Right now Valerie has lots of questions about God. Maybe you do, too. You may be wondering if God is really good, and if so, where he was when you got humiliated in front of the whole soccer team. Maybe you're doubting there really is a God, after all.

If you're doubting God, you're not alone. Did you know that all throughout history, people have doubted his presence and goodness? Job and his wife certainly did, when God allowed all of Job's riches and children to be taken away. In the book of Psalms, David tells how he felt, hiding away in the desert, when King Saul was trying to kill him. Sometimes he felt as if God had left him out in the cold (or, in this case, in the heat) all alone. Doubting Thomas definitely didn't believe Jesus had risen from the dead; he thought the Messiah was dead and gone.

DOUBT OR DISBELIEF?

Is it wrong to question God? Does it cause you to lose your faith? The answer is a big NO. But there are two kinds of doubt: good doubt and bad doubt. What's the difference?

Good doubt leads you to ask questions of God so that you grow to understand him and love him more. Job asked God why all the bad things were happening to him, but he never lost faith in God's presence or goodness. And, in the end, he praised God for the bad things because they brought him closer to God:

> But [God] knows the way that I take;
>> when he has tested me, I will come forth as gold.
> My feet have closely followed his steps;
>> I have kept to his way without turning aside.
> *Job 23:10-11*

But that's not how his wife felt. She had the bad doubts big time. Bad doubt means you don't want to believe in God because if God is real, then you have to fix whatever's wrong in your life. So you come up with lots of reasons to doubt his very existence and goodness.

ARE YOU REALLY THERE?

When's the last time you doubted God's existence or goodness? Tell about it:

_____

_____

What kind of doubt was it—good or bad? Why?

_____

_____

When you feel like Jesus is letting you down, talk to him about it. Admit honestly, "God, sometimes I find it hard to believe you're there. Please help me to believe that you're good and that you love me and care about what happens to me."

No matter what you feel like from day to day, always keep Jesus' promise in mind:

> Do not let your hearts be troubled. Trust in God; trust also in me.
>
> *John 14:1*

Jesus is the only One who *always* keeps his word.

DAY THREE
THAT'LL NEVER HAPPEN TO ME

POW! Todd laid a heavy blow on his punching bag. *They can't do this to me! It's not fair, God!* he yelled inside. And yet he wasn't surprised. Ever since he could remember, his mom and dad hadn't gotten along very well. But he had always thought they'd stay together.

Even when his friend Jonathan's parents were divorced, Todd never imagined that it could happen to him. Somehow dealing with Jonathan's parents' divorce seemed a lot easier than dealing with his own parents' divorce.

WHAMMIES

Todd and Jonathan aren't the only ones who get hit with whammies. Lots of times you might wonder where God is, especially when something bad happens to you. Whammies happen all the time—not making the volleyball team, your sister getting in a car wreck, your dad losing his job, slamming your finger in your locker. Big or little, they seem HUGE when they happen to you. They may hurt your body, your mind, or your feelings.

WHAMMY CONTROL

When you feel God has dealt you a whammy, how do you deal with it? Do you get mad, punch your pillow, yell at your mom, turn your back on your best friend?

God has a better way of handling the bad stuff. He wants you first to cry to him for help. In the Old Testament, when David was running away from his bad problem (the king who wanted to kill him), he cried out to God:

> Hear my cry, O God; listen to my prayer.
> From the ends of the earth I call to you,
>   I call as my heart grows faint;
>   lead me to the rock that is higher than I.
> For you have been my refuge,
>   a strong tower against the foe.
> I long to dwell in your tent forever
>   and take refuge in the shelter of your wings.
> For you have heard my vows, O God;
>   you have given me the heritage of
>   those who fear your name.
> *Psalm 61:1-5*

GOOD STUFF, BAD STUFF

No matter what happens to you, God is in control. He doesn't cause the bad things that happen to you, but he does allow them. Why? God values choice. He's given us the freedom—and the responsibility—to choose how we'll react to the bad stuff. As we're forced to face our problems, we learn more of what God wants us to learn. And he has the power to bring good from the bad stuff, no matter what it is!

Why doesn't God just wipe out all the bad stuff so we don't have to face it? If it was up to us, none of us would choose anything bad—and we wouldn't learn anything either. God uses good stuff and bad stuff to help us become the persons he wants us to be.

When did something bad happen to you? (Or is it happening now?) What good stuff can you remember eventually coming out of it?

_____

_____

Ask God to help you trust him—in good times *and* in bad times.

DAY FOUR
CAREER STEER

Corinne leaned back in her chair and stared out the window. Sometimes she wished she could just escape somewhere— anywhere where no one could find her.

Since it was her senior year, everyone had high expectations of her. Her parents wanted her to go to a Christian college; her favorite teacher wanted her to go to a university and major in literature; her friends wanted her to go to the community college where they were going. Corinne didn't know what she wanted to do. She was sick of school in a big way—she couldn't *imagine* studying for four more years.

When she'd mentioned getting a job to her parents, they had freaked out, as if she were some sort of mental midget. They made it seem like her whole life would be ruined if she didn't go to school next year. She felt trapped.

THE BIG QUESTION
High-school seniors aren't the only ones who wonder what they should do with their lives. Maybe you feel like you aren't good at anything—you can't imagine what kind of job you could ever get. You wonder if God will ever show you what you're good at.

HUH?
So, how do you know what you should do? You hear all these things about "following God's will," but what does that phrase really mean? How are you supposed to know what God wants you to do?

Sometimes God may show you directly what he wants you to do (for instance, you won't get accepted at one of the colleges you applied for, and you'll get a scholarship at the other). Other times, he wants you to sort it out on your own, and you know what? He won't leave you—*kerplunk!*—with no help. His Word, the Bible, is a guide that shows us how to live our lives. Although it won't say, "You're supposed to go to Central College," or "You should be a medical doctor," it will give you general principles about how to live life God's way.

If you wonder what you should do, stack your questions up against the apostle Paul's rule for living:

> I'm not trying to be a people pleaser! No, I am trying to please God. If I were still trying to please people, I would not be Christ's servant.
> *Galatians 1:10, NLT*

What's Paul saying? That when we make decisions, we affect others around us as well. God wants us to please him first and live as examples for those who don't know him by the way we act and speak. Did you know that you're a living, walking mirror of God on earth?

DECISIONS, DECISIONS . . .

What tough life decisions are you facing soon, or sometime this year or next?

_____

_____

When you start to feel stressed out about your future, read Galatians 1:10 again. Decide if you are trying to please God—or yourself, your parents, etc. If you're trying to please God, he gives you a promise, "Commit to the LORD whatever you do, and your plans will succeed" (Proverbs 16:3). Wow! That's not a bad success ratio. Thank him today for all the surprising and wonderful things he's going to do—through you.

DAY FIVE
SURPRISE ENDINGS

Hey, thanks for . . . uh . . . just listening to me yesterday," Frank blurted out.

Darrell couldn't believe his ears. "Yeah, sure," he replied, "no big deal." But it really was a big deal. Darrell had been bummin' because he wasn't good at anything. He was just average—nothing special. He even got tongue-tied when he tried to talk with other teens about *anything,* much less Christ. How could God ever use him?

Darrell always knew he was a good listener, but somehow that didn't seem very important. Suddenly it all made sense. God had created him to help people out by listening to their problems. He could do that very easily.

Cool! he mouthed softly. *Thanks a lot, God!*

MOVIN' ON AND UP
Encouragement is something we all need, and God knows it. He even knew it back in Old Testament times. Take Joshua, for example. The first time we hear about him, he's forty and he's been chosen to go on a secret spying mission to the Promised Land. You know, check things out and make sure it's okay before the rest of the Israelites storm in by the thousands (and get blown up by enemy land mines or something—at least that's how the movies go, right?).

Then later we see him as an older man (probably in his eighties). He had just become the leader of the Israelites after the great Moses. We're sure he was thinking, "Me, God? You want *me* to lead all these people? I can't do it!" But God gave him these words to carry in his heart:

As I was with Moses, so I will be with you; I will never leave you nor forsake you.

Be strong and courageous, because you will lead these people to inherit the land I swore to their forefathers to give them. Be strong and very courageous. Be careful to obey all the law my servant Moses gave you; do not turn from it to the right or to the left, that you may be successful wherever you go. Do not let this Book of the Law depart from your mouth; meditate on it day and night, so that you may be careful to do everything written in it. Then you will be prosperous and successful. Have I not commanded you? Be strong and courageous. Do not be terrified; do not be discouraged, for the LORD your God will be with you wherever you go.

Joshua 1:5-9

Even though Joshua was old compared to you, he still had a self-esteem problem. God had to tell him three times to "be strong and courageous" in order to get the message through his thick head!

GOD'S CALLING YOU

God still calls each one of us today, just as he did Joshua. Maybe not to be leaders of a great nation like Israel, but to be a friend to someone who needs one. But he doesn't want to *make* us do it. He wants us to be willing to do what he gives us to do. And he wants us to be willing to accept his teaching, through the words of the Bible. If we will do that, and live our lives God's way, he promises that we'll have a wonderful ending—that never ends!

For the grace of God that brings salvation has appeared to all. . . . It teaches us to say "No" to ungodliness and worldly passions, and to live self-controlled, upright and godly lives in this present age, while we wait for the blessed hope—the glorious appearing of our great God and Savior, Jesus Christ, who gave himself for us to redeem us from all wickedness and to purify for himself a

people that are his very own, eager to do what is good.
Titus 2:11-14

God freely gives the choice of eternal life to each one of us, but he leaves the choosing up to you. By *not* choosing, you also make a choice—for the dark, dismal future of hell. But if you choose God's way, you'll have a wonderful eternal surprise. Boy, we can't wait to unwrap ours!

THE BALL'S IN YOUR COURT

What do you look forward to in the future?

_____

_____

If you're a Christian—if you believe Jesus is your personal Savior and died on the cross for your sins, and you've accepted that sacrifice—you have a choice to make today. Will you live to please your friends, parents, teachers, etc., or will you choose to please Christ in all you say and do?

If you're not sure you're a Christian, today's the day to secure your eternal future. It's either heaven or hell. Jesus is begging you to make your decision today. What'll it be? Why not make today the day you pray this simple prayer:

> *Jesus, I believe you're God's Son—and that you died on the cross for my sins. I accept that sacrifice. I'm sorry for all the bad things I've done, and I ask your forgiveness. Come into my heart and live with me. Help me to do what's right and to grow as a Christian as I walk with you. And thank you for your promise of eternal life in heaven with you! Amen.*

ABOUT THE AUTHORS

JEFF AND RAMONA TUCKER have over thirty years of combined ministry experience with junior high and high school students. Jeff is a plant superintendent at a manufacturing facility and Ramona is the editor of *Today's Christian Woman* magazine. They live in Chicago, Illinois.